Carla Lane is best known for her work as a writer for television. Her series, which include: *The Liver Birds*, *Butterflies* and *Bread*, are classics of their genre. It is less widely known that Carla is also a writer of poetry. This selection brings together both her astute observations on life and her passion for animals.

The proceeds from the sale of this book will be donated to the West Sussex animal sanctuary: Animaline.

Web address http://www.animaline.org.uk

DREAMS AND OTHER AGGRAVATIONS

Selected Poems

by

CARLA LANE

Consultant Editor

Stevie Davies

Earth Ventures

First published in 2003 by
EARTH VENTURES
Broadhurst Manor
Horsted Keynes, Haywards Heath
West Sussex RH17 7BG
www.carlalane.com/earthventures

E-mail: earthventures@carlalane.com

ISBN 0-9543673-0-8

Acknowledgements

Acknowledgement is due to the following publications in which some of these poems first appeared:

Pool, published by The Oasis Group, Liverpool (1978). *Instead of Diamonds* by Carla Lane, published by Michael Joseph Ltd. (1995), and by Penguin Books Ltd. (1996). *Wide Prairie*: Album released by MPL Communications Ltd. (1998).

My thanks go to Steve and Barby for their friendship and support, and to Stevie Davies for her generous help and guidance.

Thanks also to John Sansom, of Sansom & Company (Bristol), for his advice and assistance.

Contents

DREAMS AND OTHER AGGRAVATIONS

To the memory of Linda McCartney
and the times we spent

I turn to the company of animals
when my spirit hangs its head

Cow

Placid creature,
Standing in your June field,
With one more day of grazing
Before the slatted truck.

And when it comes
You will go — with quiet dignity,
Across the yard, up the ramp,
Into the dark.

Trusting creature,
Going to meet the final man,
With nothing on your face
Except for that familiar beauty.
And he will eat you,
Because he didn't look.
He didn't look.

Lady Linda
Requiem for Linda McCartney

They scoffed in the beginning, didn't they.
Cranks they called us,
But you took the path where no-one had gone:
You promised them a voice,
And you held their terror close.
There was no lowly creature in your eye,
No size, no strength, no special beauty,
They were all the same.
And finally, your shout drowned out
The less committed sounds,
Until it was heard in the people's conscience.
And it rose above the sceptics,
The cruelty makers, the money takers,
And it settled in the hearts of many.
You left a trail and others will follow that trail,
The one you trod so passionately.
We will complete your journey.
It will not be easy, it will be long because
Before peace and dignity can come to the animals,
It must come to man.
Lady Linda, we cannot see you,
But we still hear you.

Sheep

I am only a sheep
I eat and I sleep,
Not like you,
But my way.

I hear sounds and I know
When they are kind.
It is hard sometimes
A safe place to find,
From you.

I know pain and fear
When harsh words I hear,
And my heart goes fast,
Like you.

I know peace in the sun,
I can jump,
I can run,
Like you.

And I know the cost
When my lamb is lost,
And I suffer many times
Not like you,
But quietly — like me.

Goose

She was just a goose
Drifting loose,
Away from the rest,
Because in her chest,
A pellet of lead.

I held her close
As he prepared the dose,
And close to my face,
Resting there,
Her magnificent head.

I could smell her river,
Hear the willows shiver,
See the pulsing sky
Trapped in her eye,
And there she was,
Finished.

Lament

Dear Lord, dear sky, dear star, dear tree,
Whatever, wherever, whoever you be,
Gift us with far-reaching minds
And a compassionate soul, whatever we find
At the end of the trail, where blood runs deep,
And fear-filled animals meet their last sleep.
Bring soon the day, dear Lord, dear songbird, dear
    sound-of-the-herd,
When man will unite, take up the fight
For them, our companions of sun and shower.
Bring nearer, dear Lord, dear river, dear flower,
Bring nearer an end to their terror and pain,
Bring nearer their safety, bring nearer our shame.

Granddad

My first poem — aged 8

Despair not for him,
Let sadness grow dim,
And when sweet birds call
Smile and recall.

My Granny's Bucket

In the cobbled yard, where the sun played
And insects hung like bits of silk
Above the marigolds,
I heard my granny's bucket
As she scrubbed the step and brought it white with
    stone.
The canary sat in its brass cage
Like a perfect powder puff,
Now and then pausing to watch the visiting bee
As it passed between the bars
On its way to the window box.
Soft stirrings, beneath stones, amongst ivy, by the
    old tap,
Things which fluttered and crawled, unmolested,
In the cobbled yard
To the sound of my granny's bucket.

Arthritic City

I'm getting near you now, Arthritic City,
I can smell the stone caves near the station,
And soon the steel umbrella of Lime Street,
Taxis like rows of black beetles
Taking our Mary there,
Me Dad here,
And Aunty Cissy into the blossoming suburbs,
Away from your cobblestone soul,
Distancing them from the great docks,
Where ships waited, and grandfathers came ashore
    with their spoils,
And as the red brick and the grey stone,
The wrought iron, the slates and the bells grew black
    with time,
The city planners sat in their sterile offices
Planning the cosmetic surgery,
A lift here, a tuck there,
And during the surgical dig
Your guts took refuge in children unborn.

My Gran

My gran sits out there,
By the front door in her old brown chair
On her face there is no trace of now.
Her folded skin and lips gone thin
Speak only of yesterday,
Of ribbons, and silk, white lace,
And the summer sound of cows being milked.
My gran has new red slippers,
And a soft warm shawl,
And she pretends to be asleep
When Mrs Bramley calls.
'Hello love,' then whispering,
'It's a shame when they are old
They don't bother much
And they keep catching cold,
It's an empty time.'
But my gran is remembering a travelling stream
Where frogs did live and fish did gleam.
Where foxglove and lavender wildly grew,
And the woodman's cart came trundling through.
My gran has a wide gold band
Shining on her arthritic hand,
And in closed eyes, hidden there,
Soft memories of her wedding prayer.
She hasn't time for idle talking,
She hasn't the legs for blessed walking
But in her head all things grow,
And no-one knows what my gran knows.

Liverpool Lament

He pursued me gently — with dignity
Thrush-like
Said he loved me desperately
With his heart, and such like
He kissed me and held me
Shy, and boy like
I trembled beside him
Soft and coy like
Not long after, I became all sick like
So he went back to his wife
Quick like

Myxomatosis

Little rabbit hardly grown
With swollen face and eyes gone
When you finally stop
And when spring calls again
Will your-kind return
Healed and forgiving
Or will you bestow on those thoughtless mindless
    soulless bastards who caused it all
The gift of extinction

The Jolly Farmer

1994: Fred the jolly farmer
Was making lots of dough,
With set aside and subsidies,
Off to the pub he'd go.
Evenin' Jack.
Evenin' Fred.
Now here's the general picture,
If we buy more stock, and fill our sheds,
We could be even richer.

Ooh ah, aye ah,
Oh for the life of a farmer.

1998: Fred the jolly farmer
Was losing lots of dough,
His barns were just a-bursting,
And prices very low.
Evenin' Fred.
Evenin' Jack.
Up all night I've been,
Me wife has gone, me sheep are sick,
I haven't got a bean,
The grass is wet, there's no more hay,
It's the worst I've ever seen.

Ooh ah, aye ah,
Woe is the life of a farmer.

1999: I'll tell you what, said farmer Joe,
      Don't give yourself the judders,
      The animal ship is sailing soon,
      So just don't feed the buggers.
      No-one can tell they could be from hell,
      There's nothing in their ears,
      So off they go with a ho, ho, ho,
      Cheers, cheers, cheers.

      Ooh ah, aye ah.
      What a jolly plan.

2000: Farmer Jack and Fred and Joe
      Are in The Fox and Hounds.
      Outside, three new Discoveries
      Are parked within the grounds.
      Cheers, said Jack. Cheers, said Joe.
      Cheers, said Farmer Fred.
      I thought it up when me last sheep dropped,
      And I was lying in me bed.
      Do not panic — go organic,
      Was the thought inside me head.

      You've got the land, you've got the tractor,
      All you need is a bucket of seed
      And a touch of the 'feel good' factor.
      Well done Fred, the others said,
      And they banged with joy on the table.
      Who's to know, said Farmer Joe,
      That it's only on the label?

      Ooh ah, aye ah,
      How jolly to be a farmer!

Thoughts

Think of the plight of the fox in flight
The beasts in the slaughterhouse
Hear their call as the hunted fall
And the cry of the scientist's mouse

The White-Coated Man

Song about Vivisection

Through the bars the morning light
What is this feeling, why can't I move?

Sometime today they'll set me free,
I'll hear a voice and it will be my friend,
The white-coated man.

Where is the wind? Where are the leaves?
What happened — why this pain?

Sometime today they'll set me free,
I'll hear a voice and it will be my friend,
The white-coated man.

If man wants life and eternity,
Then man must pay and man must see
That we are theirs to mind,
For man is the voice, man is the law,
If man gets sick he'll find a cure, our friend,
The white-coated man.

In the distance people are laughing,
Do they know about me, why can't I see?

And they will pay, the silent ones,
The silent ones will pay.

The Slaughterhouse

A place where the eye of the innocent
Meets the eye of the betrayer
And the excellence of man is diminished

The Quiet Man

A man must have fun
Said the man with the gun,
Do what he needs to do.
So the pheasants fall — after all
That's what guns are meant to do.
 'Right,' said the quiet man.

I spotted a vixen the other day
Lively thing I have to say.
The lamp was bright — caught her eye
Hello fox — Goodbye.
 'Right,' said the quiet man.

Feel the metal — feel the wood
Makes a sporting man feel good.
Take it — try it — there's a crow,
Blast him high, he won't even know.
Ah there's a rabbit — feel the joy,
Get the habit.
 'Right,' said the quiet man.

These animal people are soft in the head,
We're all alive — we'll all be dead.
So do your thing — have some fun,
You haven't lived till you've raised a gun.
 'Right,' said the quiet man.
So he shot him.

Me

I'm quite good at climbing a moderate incline,
I can run with the dog and bring logs for the fire,
I can ride on a bike and can handle a boat,
As long as it's small and sets sail in a moat.
I can chase my cat when she catches a rat,
I can outwit the wind when he wisps off my hat,
I can climb the stairs be they moderate or steep,
I can fetch out the hay for the goats and the sheep,
I can argue wildly and defeat my opponents,
About life, and love and Hoover components.
I can put on the charm and turn a man's head,
Pretend to be helpless and I'm quite good in bed.
I can make a grand speech in front of the masses,
But I can never find my bloody glasses.

Sons

Little bits of me
Splintered in a glance
Imprisoned in the eye
Friends of my womb
Going out of the house
Like tall gods smiling
With my smile
Nothing you do
Surprises me
Because I knew you before you were born
And I loved you long before then

Family

You are all here
Young
Noisy
Stealing my time with the problems of your youth
Not remembering that mine has gone
And that is my problem
Could you, just for today
Take your smiles, and your restless limbs
Your music, and your lovers
Who fill my house with nowhere to go
And separate my mind from all that grows there
Could you, just for today
Make me a gift of loneliness

If You Were Dead

If you were dead
I'd long to see you.
I would wander through yesterday's places,
Aching,
I would carry your face
In my eye.
I would see nothing else,
And all of me would be
Breaking.

If you were dead,
There would be
A death in me,
And I'd feel your touch,
Endlessly.
I would worship your pillow,
And dream in your chair,
I would hug your cat,
Let him sleep in my hair,
But you're not dead,
You are alive,
And I hate you.

Go Now

Go now — the way you do,
The angry glare, the helpless stare.
It's nearly done, and one by one —

The reprisals, then the ritual,
Bed — nothing left to do,
The final fuck.
Go now — the way you do.

When I Am Old

When youth has gone,
And I struggle on
With my assorted ills
And my potions and pills,
When the breasts you adore
Reach for the floor,
And my tired face
Hangs like lace
In the window of life,
Will you turn away
And think of the day
When eyes shone clear
And silk days were here?
Will mist and memory crowd your head
As we creak and clatter in our lovers' bed,
Or will you reach out
And stifle the scream?

Happiness

It doesn't stay
It hasn't time to follow me
As I hurry with my sorrow
Through another day
It doesn't wait by my bed
Like the mottled kitten
Or sing in my hair
Like August
It is always — just ahead
Or just behind
It doesn't stay

Old Cat (Wolfgang)

You sleep a lot now, deep, impenetrable sleep, your
paled green eyes are hidden, but how bright they
were — how soft your ginger fur, and your white
paws, like little socks tucked beneath your chin.

Soon when feed dishes clatter you will jump awake,
and without a faltering step you will plod steadily to
the plate, faint snoring sounds as you eat, and as you
go back to your bed, the limping returns, and the
'miaow' which is never now complete, and the
painful ritual of washing your face, before you
return to sleep, where you will sit in sunny places
and take butterflies by surprise.

Dear old cat, we have journeyed through so many
days of colour and blackness, we have grieved the
loss of others of our kind, we have walked in wind-
tossed woodlands and stretched in silent grass. Stay
with me, I will walk with you where once you ran,
and your every pause to rest will be my pause, and I
will answer your every weakened call and when you
are gone, wherever I go there will be a moment in
my day, when I will see you clearly running toward
me, beloved old cat.

Pandora

Dear sweet cat with your surprised eyes and sunlit
    fur,
What joy to lie beneath the tree, with you singing in
    my hair.

Remember Maximus

There are moments when the umbrella of sorrow
   hangs over me.
I question the chaffinch's song,
And there seems to be no reason for the buttercups.

The Lane

Today, in the lane where I walk
Everything is dying its November death
Trees fall into their black sleep
Leaves cling
Like finished men
About to be hanged by winter
And silently
The hogweed builds her pale acropolis

Stray Dog

I took him on a lead:
He wasn't mine,
Though he chose my doorstep on which to whine.
I looked in all directions,
Avoided eye connections,
Then took him to the dogs' home and filled in the
    form about him.
Male — young — no collar —
And I walked away.
He wasn't mine.

In the yard, I hesitated:
I could hear his loneliness,
Sense the scars of other times.
I closed the metal gates and I heard keys turn.
His wail was lost now,
Gone to join the rest.
Oh God, why me,
Why not next door or Number Nine?

The following day, I looked through the bars —
That was it — he was mine.

Old Man and Old Dog

They walk together
In a shadowy lane
His legs slightly bowed
She with matching limp
Grey temple
Grey muzzle
Blue eyes and brown
Both mottled now with time
The man stops catches his breath
The dog looks up
Waiting, worrying
Then off they go through the wooden gate
Towards the old farmhouse
Where once they moved swiftly
Brown hands black paws
Man and dog
Leaping joyfully
And even now in the shadowy lane, as one

White Bird

What do you see white bird
As you go from your winter to spring
Did you see the green leaves turning brown
Did you see the great trees falling down
Did you feel man's breath on your wing
What did you hear white bird
As you moved from sky to sky

Did you hear the sound of forests burning
Did you see the great whale in his final turning
And were you in time for the river's last sigh
Before it turned yellow before it ran dry
And will you come back to a place which you know
Or will your sun-laden fields wear a halo of snow

Bindweed

You remind me of bindweed
Twisting and turning around me
Smothering me with your needs
And just as my patience reaches its final hour
You say something beautiful
And suddenly — the flower

Truth

Today I was beautiful
The taxi-driver said it
The man in the café smiled it
The boy in the lift thought it
The telephone rang it
And now I stand
Awaiting the final compliment
The day must be over
The mirror is silent

Gone

You almost made me love you,
With your secret look and your boy's hair,
But something moved behind your smile.
Was she still there?

You always denounced her,
With your trembling lip
And your practised shrug,
But it was there in your eye,
The lie.

I'm glad I didn't show it,
The gathering joy — the looking forward,
The waiting for the end of a traitor's smile,
And in its place — a lover's sigh.
And now it has come — she has truly gone.
But so have I.

The Telephone

Don't just sit there
Plastic clapometer of my popularity
Joy bringer
Fear maker
Silent assassin of my ego
Don't just sit there
Ring!

Conversation

I would like to talk to you
With my body
Not a long conversation
I wouldn't stay all night
Just a sentence or two
About the whether
Whether we should
Or whether we shouldn't

True Love

I love the way you say my name
And how you hold me
And how you get upset
Because it's raining on your car
I love that too

I love the little secret message
Your face sends across a busy room
And the way you wake up in the morning
That same face all crushed and undone
Then the smile that puts it all together again
I love that too

And when it rains
I love the way you shield me with your coat
And you keep telling my dog to sit
Even though he won't
I love the good, I love the bad
Whether you stand or fall
I love every little thing you do
But, darling, best of all —
I love chocolate

Meetings

This time, I'll tell her
Thought the man
As he trod her road
The one which led to her room
The one with pavements, the colour of his childhood
And the dead tree
Which blossomed yellow in his mind
This time I'll tell her
He followed the stairway
The narrow, growing narrower stairway
With its sudden door
And its 'ring once, ring three times' bell
No more of this
Thought the man.
She stood
Secret in the folds of night
His hand found the eggshell face
And wandered on its warm way
Down, down, into the silk trap
Next time I'll tell her
Thought the man

Eros

In the darker days of man,
Before compassion began
To educate his heart,
Seep into his bones and swell his soul with
    understanding,
There still dwelt love —
Love from the man to the girl —
Love from the girl to the man.
Before compassion began,
There was the glance,
The upheaval of sanity,
As two bloods quickened and the sweet flow of
    calamity began,
Even in the darkest days of man,
Before all reasoning things began,
There was love.

Frustrations of An Ordinary Man

I'm bloody angry, my blood runs hot,
On account of that bloody 'export' lot,
Taking our pigs, our sheep, our goats,
Over to France in a shitty boat.

Be it hot or be it cold —
Their bloody pockets stuffed with gold.
Red-faced, fat-bellied, nothing in their head,
They torture the beast until he is dead.

Bloody Belgium, Italy and Spain,
High-rise trucks with their cargo of pain.
I'll tell you something, one bloody day,
I'll be out of my bed and on my way —
Down to the docks, that place of strife
And I'll stop those bastards
If it costs me my life.

Little Bird

Little bird
Full of feather
Full of song
Full of weather
Full of joy
Full of flight
Full of day
Full of night
Full of living
Full of flying
Full of poison
Full of dying

Death on the Road

I don't know what you were,
You're just blood and tissue
On the road,
Neither feather nor fur.
Perhaps you lived
After the first pain.
Perhaps in your animal way you felt hope,
But they didn't stop,
So you waited.
And when they came with the second pain
There was blackness,
And everything carried on as normal after that.

Piggy

This little piggy went to market,
This piggy hid in a loft,
This little piggy went wee, wee, wee,
Right under a bus —
    Cos he knew he'd be better off!

Dear Pig

Dear pig
You are the less talked about
Less thought about
And the more harmed
Than all the rest

Guinea Pig

I don't expect them to understand,
After all, you're only a guinea pig,
And I'm standing here — by the cherry tree,
With the hole made,
And the little parcel of your body, clasped.
Didn't we know each other well, little friend,
Didn't we?

From Sorrow to Rage

Silly puss
Hit by a bus
Devastated us
Thoughtless cat
Doing that
Splat! Splat!

How I miss you
To hug and to kiss you
God's curse on the bus
And all buses
And on the driver
And all bus drivers

God's curse on all those who travel by bus
On the people who work in the bus depot
Especially the manager
And the people who design and assemble and paint
    buses
And the people who stand in bush shelters
May they shrivel and die

Beloved cat
Beloved puss
Squashed flat
By a fucking bus

Another World
Song

The sands are shifting
The clouds are lifting
We've heard your silence
And we're coming your way
Voices are ringing
The song we're singing is different now

The message is clear now
Your moment's here now
We've heard your silence
And we're coming your way
A new day is calling
The song we're singing is stronger now

The hand that harms will not rise again
So lift your head
cos we're coming your way

They are: the spirits of field and sky and water
of earth and branches so high

let's walk with them
let's learn from them
let's feel for them

the other children of the world
the other children of the world
the other children of the world

The winds are shifting
The clouds are lifting
We've heard your silence
And we're coming your way
Minds are awaking
The sound we are making is different now

The hand that harms will not rise again
So lift your head
cos we're coming your way

They are: the spirits of field and sky and water
of earth and branches so high

let's walk with them
let's learn from them
let's feel for them

the other children of the world
the other children of the world
the other children of the world

They are: the spirits of field and sky and water
of earth and branches so high

let's walk with them
let's learn from them
let's feel for them

the other children of the world
the other children of the world
the other children of the world

Another Thought

The advantage of being old in this troubled world is
that when you came in, everything was acceptable,
and you'll be going out before it becomes
unbearable.